FIFTY
FEMINIST
MANTRAS

A YEARLONG PRACTICE
FOR CULTIVATING FEMINIST
CONSCIOUSNESS

Amelia Hruby

Andrews McMeel
PUBLISHING®

Andrews McMeel Publishing
a division of Andrews McMeel Universal
1130 Walnut Street, Kansas City, Missouri 64106

www.andrewsmcmeel.com

20 21 22 23 24 SDB 10 9 8 7 6 5 4 3 2 1

ISBN: 978-1-5248-5882-7

Library of Congress Control Number: 2020934875

Cover Design and Illustrations by Emily Jaynes

Editor: Charlie Upchurch
Art Director/Designer: Diane Marsh
Production Editor: David Shaw
Production Manager: Tamara Haus

ATTENTION: SCHOOLS AND BUSINESSES
Andrews McMeel books are available at quantity discounts with bulk purchase for educational, business, or sales promotional use. For information, please e-mail the Andrews McMeel Publishing Special Sales Department: specialsales@amuniversal.com.

TO YOUR FEMININE SELF,
YOUR FEMINIST POTENTIAL,
AND EVERY WOMAN* WHO'S
INSPIRED OR SUPPORTED
YOU ALONG THE WAY.

*Anytime I say "woman" or "women" in this book, I mean anyone who identifies as a woman or with communities of women. I also mean the socially constructed, structurally oppressed position that produces concrete experiences of discrimination and marginalization for women. The spelling "womxn" would also be an appropriate descriptor.

CONTENTS

INTRODUCTION

On Halloween of 2016, I started a project that I named Feminist Mantra Monday. The idea was to create a weekly mantra series that would help people of all genders embrace feminisms and themselves as feminists. So each Monday for a year (with a few exceptions, of course), I posted a mantra on my Instagram profile and a brief essay explaining its meaning and feminist potential on my blog.

In many ways, the project was a public journaling process. The mantras were fueled by my activities and reflections from the week prior, often in response to things happening in the world at large. In other ways, however, the project took its own shape and form as readers invested their lives and meanings in the mantras and shared comments and conversations on the posts.

The mantras were always a self-exploratory prompt, but a community also blossomed around them. Originally published on the heels of the 2016 presidential election, they became a collective rallying cry against the election of a sexist, white supremacist president. As years passed and I continued writing weekly feminist mantras, they served as a reminder of the importance of activism and self-care and a signpost of the necessity of developing our deeply personal but always political feminist practices.

Reading and working with the feminist mantras in this book will not provide you with a detailed history of the feminist movement or a critical analysis of feminist theory. But the book will teach you some of the feminist values that I've learned by studying feminism and interviewing feminist activists for the past seven years.

These values are communicated through important lessons in trusting your intuition, learning to listen, cultivating community bonds, nurturing our emotions and desires, reconsidering the role of the feminine, and imagining futures for ourselves radically different from the ones provided by the white supremacist, capitalist, patriarchal society in which we live.

I believe that these lessons represent important feminist values like empathy, community, imagination, pleasure, joy, and soft power that you will learn about over the course of the mantras. As you read, I invite you to consider your own list of values and why each entry on your list may or may not be feminist. Each of us will arrive at our own answers, and I encourage you to treat this book as an invitation for your own reflection rather than a guide to the right answers.

The intention of this book is to make space for each of us to continue (or to begin) a weekly feminist mantra practice in our lives. I encourage you to set aside a time each week to read and meditate on one of the mantras.

They are arranged in the book by season, but feel free to skip weeks that don't resonate with you and come back when they do. There are structured journal pages with each mantra to help you reflect on how it may apply to your life and the lives of others. Sometimes these pages are just a few simple questions; other times they will guide you through creative exercises. Again, sit with or skip these prompts as feels right to you.

If you make posts about the mantras or the book on your social profiles, feel free to tag them with #FiftyFeministMantras. I'm also still posting new feminist mantras on Instagram every

Monday, and you can join the community following those at #FeministMantraMonday.

If you want to connect off Instagram, I produce a podcast called *Fifty Feminist States* where I travel across the United States interviewing feminist activists and artists. It's a great way to learn more about the grassroots feminist work happening around the country and to consider how your feminist mantra practice can support community organizing efforts.

As you can see, there are myriad ways to be in touch, so please don't hesitate to reach out if you'd like to share about your journey. It brings me true joy to take part in your feminist self-exploration and community creation, and I'm so excited to cheer you on through your journey. I hope this practice brings you greater insight into your feminine self, your feminist potential, and past, present, and future communities of women.

Always,

Amelia @ameliajohruby
ameliahruby.com

A NOTE ABOUT MANTRAS

Some of you may not be familiar with the idea of mantras and their purpose. Most generally, mantras are words or phrases meant to be repeated to help you focus and concentrate. They are similar to intentions or guiding principles or very short prayers.

Each of the mantras in this book is just one or a few words long, and all of them start with verbs. The idea is that meditating on them will help them sink into your mind and heart, and then they will help guide your actions throughout the week. I find that in moments of stress or confusion, my weekly mantra can help me feel grounded in navigating our busy, complex world and making decisions that are true to myself.

There are many ways to develop a mantra practice. Some people like to meditate on their mantra each morning before they get out of bed. Others put a Post-it note on their mirror or make it their phone background so that they see it many times a day. Some prefer to light a candle and journal about it once at the beginning of the week and then let it linger in their subconscious until the next week's mantra meditation.

I encourage you to craft a mantra practice that suits you and allows the mantras to best serve you. You may follow the writing prompts I give or make up your own as you go. There is no wrong way to use a mantra, and a mantra should always feel nourishing and supporting.

WINTER

i. **BEGIN**

The start of something new is always an opportunity to begin. And a beginning, in some sense, is always a birth. It takes us back to the moments of our lives before we remember ourselves. It connects us to our mothers and the terrifying-glorifying moments of leaving a womb for the world. It represents a radical opening to possibility.

But as radical as any beginning may be, we never really get a clean break from everything that's come before. Our history—the history of our lives, of our ancestors' lives, of our society's lives—is always with us.

Every beginning holds many pasts, presents, and futures. Every beginning holds even more ends. This can be profoundly exciting and overwhelming, simultaneously.

If you're sitting down with this book, then you've decided that something about this time will be intentional.

You will carve out space for yourself. You will seek and shape your identity. You will recognize that that work happens amid the challenging structures and systemic issues we face in the world.

Those tasks begin today. This beginning is an invitation to cultivate feminist consciousness through feminist values and the study of feminist mantras. It is an opening to new, radical possibilities for yourself and our world that recognize how gender and power intermingle.

IT IS A FEMININE AND
FEMINIST REBIRTH.

As you open this book, consider: How do you feel today? Are you excited about what's to come? Spend a few moments freewriting about your feelings.

_____

_____

_____

_____

_____

_____

_____

_____

_____

What possibilities do you seek this year? Make a list of what you desire for yourself, then another list of what you need from the world.

_____	_____
_____	_____
_____	_____
_____	_____
_____	_____
_____	_____
_____	_____
_____	_____
_____	_____

What do you notice about what falls in each column? Are the entries different? The same? How might you connect them to each other?

_____

_____

_____

_____

_____

_____

_____

_____

From your lists of desires and needs, decide: What's one thing you can do today to seek something on your lists? Write it below as a promise to yourself.

_____

_____

_____

_____

_____

_____

_____

TRY THAT THING. TOMORROW
TRY ANOTHER. JUST BEGIN.

ii. NURTURE YOUR HEART

How often do you stop and ask yourself what your heart needs?

Not what your body needs, or what your mind tells you, but what your heart needs, what the deep red organ of your emotions desires.

This week's mantra is about embracing the side of yourself that feels profoundly, then working to articulate that profound feeling so that you can respect and heed it.

Consider: When do you feel most alive? When does your spirit overflow your body? When can you sense that surge of joy in your chest? That's your heart speaking. Make a list of as many times as you can remember when you felt your heart speak.

_____

_____

_____

_____

_____

_____

_____

_____

_____

_____

_____

_____

Now choose one of those moments and write about it in more detail. What brought it on? How did it feel exactly? Whom were you with? How long did it last?

_____

_____

_____

_____

_____

_____

_____

_____

_____

_____

_____

_____

_____

_____

_____

_____

_____

_____

Nurturing your heart is about getting in touch with these feelings so that you can identify your deepest desires and manifest them in the world. Now that you've remembered how that felt, spend some time journaling about your desires.

What do you want? Let your answer include things that immediately come to mind and things that take some time to find their way out from the depths. Keep writing until you feel like all of your desires are on the page.

_____

_____

_____

_____

_____

_____

_____

_____

_____

_____

_____

_____

_____

_____

_____

_____

For now, let that list of desires mingle and manifest. Rather than creating a plan of action for how you'll achieve or obtain what you desire, consider instead how you can listen to your heart more often so that you can keep adding to this list.

What are a few ways you can listen to your heart every day? What are a few ways you can listen to your heart today? What can you do to nurture your heart every day?

_____

_____

_____

_____

_____

_____

_____

_____

_____

_____

_____

_____

_____

_____

_____

_____

iii. **BUILD STRENGTH**

In Western society, when we think of building strength, we often immediately think of the physical body. We imagine push-ups, sprints, and physical exertion—thin bodies, toned physiques, and flat abs.

But the reality is that we build strength in many areas of our lives: physical, emotional, spiritual, intellectual. Building strength can mean lifting a heavier weight than you ever have or walking away from a relationship that you know in your gut needs to end. It can mean crafting a new meditation practice or learning a skill that has always intimidated you.

This week's task is to consider how we can build strength.

Begin by asking yourself: What events, people, places, clothes, etc., in your life make you feel strong? Which make you feel weak? Fill in the chart below with ideas for each.

things that make you feel strong	things that make you feel weak

Making this list may be a challenging task. It may make you feel good or bad or somewhere in between. Take a moment to reflect on how it felt to fill in each column.

_____

_____

_____

As you begin to work on building strength this week, the important thing to remember is that it doesn't happen all at once. Building strength is not about imagining your ideal self and then judging yourself for not being there.

Rather, building strength happens bit by bit over time until suddenly you've become strong, perhaps without noticing.

This can be hard for women (and most marginalized people), because most often we are not encouraged to be strong. We are told to be quiet or to make others' needs a priority over our own.

We are urged to accept what we are given rather than to ask for more.

Women are strong. And we can build even more strength in the upcoming months and years if we do it together.

So begin building strength by asking yourself: Is there a woman you'd like to emulate? Can her strength inspire yours? Make a list of women (real, imaginary, friends, celebrities, anyone) who you think are strong along with one reason why for each woman.

_____

_____

_____

Now that you've made your list of strong examples and icons, reconsider the strength and weakness columns you filled in about your own life.

From those lists, brainstorm areas of your life where you'd like to build strength. Maybe you feel strongest in yoga class and you want to stretch even farther. Maybe you feel weakest around a particular person and you need to set some boundaries around your interactions with them. Reflect on those moments below.

_____

_____

_____

_____

_____

_____

From these reflections, choose one area of your life where you will commit to building strength. Write it down here.

_____

_____

_____

_____

_____

_____

Your final task for today is to brainstorm a list of ways that you can build strength in that area.

Have fun with this list. Write it in your favorite pen. Fill it with as much joy as possible.

12 When you're done, circle your top three options. Tomorrow try to do one of them. By the next day, you'll be stronger.

_____

_____

_____

_____

_____

_____

_____

_____

_____

_____

_____

_____

_____

_____

_____

_____

iv. DWELL

One of the beautiful things about winter is that it is a time of hibernation and rest in preparation for bloom and blossom.

This mantra suggests that we accept and embrace winter as a waiting period that we can relish in as we quietly prepare for spring.

To do this, we first have to remember that waiting isn't static or stagnant.

Rather, waiting provides a space for stretching and reflecting. And accepting waiting is about embracing the present moment and yourself in this moment.

Waiting also has an intimate relationship with dwelling.

Dwelling sometimes has a negative connotation. We're told not to dwell on bad feelings—that spending time dwelling on something is a waste.

But we also call the places we live dwellings. We dwell in our homes and our lives. We take our time in each moment and room.

IN DWELLING,
WE EMBRACE A WAITING
THAT DEEPENS.

TAKE EXTRA TIME THIS WEEK.

Try to pause throughout your routines and linger in those everyday movements and spaces.

Envision those routines now.

Use the space below to write down what a typical day in your life looks like.

_____

_____

_____

_____

_____

_____

_____

_____

_____

_____

_____

_____

_____

_____

Looking at what you wrote, what's one moment in your day you wish you could linger in longer? How can you dwell there?

_____

_____

_____

_____

_____

_____

_____

_____

_____

How can you resist the pressures of our capitalist society to always be working on something or toward the next thing?

_____

_____

_____

_____

_____

_____

_____

_____

_____

V. FEEL IN THE DARK

Most often, it seems like we spend our time either too deep in our feelings to make sense of them or too far removed from them to think anything but sensibly.

This feeling that we can only succumb to or ignore our feelings is a symptom of patriarchy and patriarchy's emphasis on reason. We aren't taught how to sense, process, and value our emotions, so we are either overwhelmed by them or out of touch with them.

One of the challenging things about feelings is that they seem to come from some dark place inside of us that we can't make sense of. But if we can release our efforts to make sense of that dark place, then we can see that its darkness is generative, productive, and creative. It gives birth to the things we know to be most true of ourselves.

How are you feeling today? Write your answer in one or two sentences.

_____

_____

_____

_____

_____

_____

_____

Now close your eyes and ask again. Write two or three sentences more.

_____

_____

_____

_____

_____

_____

_____

_____

After writing twice, do you feel closer to or further from your emotions? Reflect below.

_____

_____

_____

_____

_____

_____

_____

_____

Now close your eyes and ask yourself how you feel again. This time, dwell in that dark place behind your eyelids. Feel through the darkness. Sense yourself there.

When you open your eyes, try to depict your emotions below without words. Draw, sketch, scribble, or just mark a color.

Now, if you like, reflect on that experience in words. What came up? Was moving toward and then away from words empowering for you? Was it terrifying? What does this tell you about the relationship between your feelings and reason?

_____

_____

_____

_____

_____

_____

_____

_____

vi. **TRUST THE PROCESS**

Contemporary society encourages us to be impatient. In our cultural narratives of progress and efficiency, we're always supposed to be doing more and doing it faster.

Often, however, life just doesn't work this way.

SO MANY THINGS HAVE TO DEVELOP SLOWLY. SO MUCH HAS TO TAKE ITS TIME.

Rather than worrying about what you're working toward this week, try to consider how you're getting there.

What are the steps you're taking and the stages you're moving through in your life right now?

_____

_____

_____

_____

_____

_____

_____

_____

_____

_____

_____

_____

What processes or habits are you building that support your goals and values?

_____

_____

_____

_____

_____

_____

_____

_____

Do you trust that your process will take you where you want to go?

_____

_____

_____

_____

_____

_____

_____

_____

Trusting the process is especially important for women, whose natural cycles and processes have been ignored or repressed for so long.

Don't let society make you believe that linear, phallic processes of progress and endless growth are the only way.

Your process may be soft, circular, and intuitive. Rather than a line, it might be a squiggle, a curve, or a swirl.

SEEK OUT YOUR CYCLE.
FIND YOUR PROCESS.
LEAN INTO IT.

Consider: How can you make each moment of your process a bit smoother, softer, more fulfilling?

_____

_____

_____

_____

_____

_____

How can you dwell in your process so that the journey becomes as lush as reaching the goal?

_____

_____

_____

_____

_____

_____

EXPAND

Somewhere in history, society became obsessed with the idea of women being small.

That idea grew from an obsession to a demand and from a demand to a rule.

Now we're at the point where it seems like women must be small. They shouldn't take up space. They should shrink themselves at all costs. The smaller, the better.

Not all women experience this in the same way or even experience it at all. But it is a societal reality that all women have to confront and that all men need to refuse to comply with.

This week's mantra is a reminder of how positive it is to expand, to fill yourself out and grow bigger, larger, downright huge if you like—not necessarily in your body but in your heart, mind, and spirit.

Women are taught to take up less space, but what if they demanded more?

Take up all the space you can find today. To practice, try one or all of the following:

- Stretch out your arms.
- Reach up over your head.
- Straighten your spine.
- Straighten your legs.
- Roll your wrists and ankles.
- Stretch your fingers and toes as wide as they'll go.
- Stand up.
- Walk with long strides.

After you're done, reflect on how you feel. Did you notice any tension or apprehension in your movements? Does your body feel differently now that you're done?

_____

_____

_____

_____

_____

_____

_____

_____

_____

_____

_____

Now that we've expanded our bodies literally, we can expand imaginatively, too.

CLOSE YOUR EYES.

IMAGINE AN OCEAN.

MAKE YOURSELF THE OCEAN.

FEEL THE POWER OF
YOUR WAVES.

SEE WHERE YOUR
CURRENT TAKES YOU.

viii. **COMFORT YOURSELF**

Part of feminist consciousness is cultivating communities of women, listening to and embracing them.

Another, equally important, part of feminist consciousness is cultivating the ability to stand on your own and feel comfortable and confident in your skin and life.

This week focus on holding on to self-care routines and rituals that heal your spirit.

Women are oftentimes told to take care of themselves last. Think about how it would feel to take care of yourself first.

Building an intimate self-love practice is vital for survival, and it will make you better prepared to love others when they need to be comforted in turn.

To begin, here's a short list of potential tools for self-comfort:

- Loose-leaf tea brewed slowly

- Mary Oliver poems

- Bouquets of eucalyptus and lavender

- New nail polish or lipstick

- Long walks that linger

- A favorite dessert

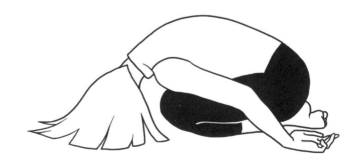

And a few particularly feminist forms of self-comfort:

- Copying Audre Lorde essays into your journal
- Listening to Patti Smith albums
- Taking self-portraits
- Having a long conversation with a woman you admire

Using these as inspiration, make your own list of comforts below. Be creative and expansive in your idea of comfort and what can create comfort for you. Here are a few prompts to help:

List something comforting for your heart, your body, and your mind.

_____

_____

List something comforting for each of your five senses.

TASTE _____

_____

TOUCH _____

_____

SMELL _____

_____

SIGHT _____

_____

SOUND _____

_____

List ways you've been comforted before.

_____

_____

_____

_____

List any other ways you can come up with to comfort yourself.

_____

_____

_____

_____

After you finish your list, ask yourself: How can you comfort yourself in the next few days? Write five ways below and consider that your to-do list for the week.

1. _____

2. _____

3. _____

4. _____

5. _____

ix. GENERATE GOODWILL

Winter often feels like a season of lean times.

But as much as we may miss the warmth of sunny days, this season is also full of moments of gathering and community, of friends and family offering encouragement and support.

In winter, we have the time and energy to spend time and energy cultivating and caring for our relationships. And when we need to call on them, those people and efforts will come back to us tenfold. There will be more goodwill than we can imagine.

To generate goodwill is to sow seeds of kindness, respect, and empathy with no expectation.

It is a refusal of the capitalist value structure that demands equal exchange, and it is the embrace of this fruitless labor that is so often labeled as feminine and ignored.

Most importantly, it is being proud of this work, valuing it and yourself, and knowing and trusting all the ways the goodwill you generate will return to you.

What can you do to generate goodwill this week?

Maybe you could check in on an elderly relative or friend, offer to walk your neighbor's dog while they're out of town, call a friend you haven't spoken to recently, or try a volunteer activity you've been putting off.

Make a list on the next page of ways you can invest time and energy in cultivating and caring for your relationships and community. When you're done, put one or two of them on your calendar this week or next.

x. **STRETCH**

Do you ever feel like everyone around you is pushing their boundaries and stepping outside their comfort zones? That you're watching the people you love stretch and grow?

Maybe some of them have taken it on voluntarily, and maybe others have been forced to try new things or new ways of doing things.

But regardless of the motive, that energy can make everything feel fresh and new.

This is one of the best things about an imminent change in seasons.

As it finally starts to feel like spring, we all start moving our bodies and stretching out again.

We make ourselves a bit uncomfortable, and we grow infinitely as a result.

WE MAKE OURSELVES A BIT UNCOMFORTABLE, AND WE GROW INFINITELY AS A RESULT.

A stretch can be a physical movement. It can be a first step. It can mean raising your voice or pressing send on a scary email. Stretching takes many forms, depending on what you're stretching toward. And what you're stretching toward may range from a raise at work to a new apartment, from a challenging recipe to just touching your toes.

This week consider:

What's one (or more) thing just out of reach that you think you can grasp?

_____

_____

_____

_____

_____

_____

How can you reach toward one of those things this week?

_____

_____

_____

_____

_____

_____

_____

Now that you're stretching, what are the things you tell yourself that you're not capable of?

_____

_____

_____

_____

_____

_____

_____

_____

_____

How can you stretch, even slightly, toward those things?

_____

_____

_____

_____

_____

_____

_____

_____

_____

_____

xi. **STAY SEASONAL**

In winter we tend to hibernate. We crave the warmth and comfort of blankets, hot beverages, and one too many nightcaps.

When the weather warms and days lighten, we crave greener foods and more outdoor activities. We fill spring full of salads and bike rides and long nights outside.

This is because you have different needs and desires in the spring than in the winter. This is important to note and to remember that "bad" or "better" decisions are bad or better only in the context of the season you're making them in and whether they suit what your body and spirit need at the time.

The productive, abstract, rational world we live in tries to demand that our lives function without care for or appeal to the seasons. For example, your boss expects you to be at work at 8 a.m. regardless of whether the sun rose at 5 a.m. or 7 a.m.

This is largely the result of a patriarchal and capitalist value system that demands we remain productive at the same rates year-round for maximum profit.

But in reality, our bodies and minds are in tune with our environments. Their needs and desires ebb and flow.

WE ARE SEASONAL BEINGS, JUST LIKE THE PLANTS, ANIMALS, AND PEOPLE WE SHARE THIS PLANET WITH.

Make a list of the desires and habits that appeal to your winter self.

_____

_____

_____

_____

_____

_____

_____

_____

Now write down how those morph into your spring self.

_____

_____

_____

_____

_____

_____

_____

_____

_____

_____

"Stay seasonal" is a reminder to listen to your body and give it what it needs with the understanding that these needs will fluctuate with the season. It's a call to tap into your feminine connection to Mother Earth.

Now that you've considered how your desires change as the seasons shift, think about how the world around you changes. How does your natural environment look and feel in winter?

_____

_____

_____

_____

_____

_____

_____

How does it look and feel in spring?

_____

_____

_____

_____

_____

_____

_____

What lessons might you be able to learn from these changes?

_____

_____

_____

_____

_____

_____

_____

_____

_____

_____

_____

_____

_____

_____

_____

_____

_____

_____

_____

_____

_____

xii. **FIND THE GOOD**

Women are often told that the only way to be strong is to be selfless and give themselves to others.

And while it's great to learn to share your gifts and care for your community, the problem with being selfless is that giving it all away is a surefire way to have nothing left to give.

Women can and should be strong, but in order to build strength, we don't need to be selfless but to be self-full.

Being self-full is giving ourselves to people, places, and things that enrich and fulfill our lives while learning to cultivate boundaries around the things that drain us with no reciprocal return.

To begin this process, this week's mantra invites you to focus on the good in your life.

TAKE A FEW MOMENTS
AND MEDITATE ON THE
GOOD THINGS THAT
HAVE HAPPENED THIS
WEEK, THIS MONTH,
OR THIS YEAR.

Maybe there is a beautiful new person in your life. Maybe you got an extra hour of sleep last night. Maybe the sun came out today.

Once a few good things have come to mind, write about them below.

_____

_____

_____

_____

_____

_____

Often the good in our lives gets covered up by negative thoughts, events, or energy. After meditating on the good, take a few moments to think of a time (recent or not) when a good thing was clouded by something bad. Write about it below.

_____

_____

_____

_____

_____

_____

_____

Now that you've revisited that instance, brainstorm three ways you could have refocused on the good.

First, write what you could have done:

I could have

_____

_____

I could have

_____

_____

I could have

_____

_____

Now turn all these statements into commitments by saying what you will do:

Next time, I will

_____

_____

Next time, I will

_____

_____

Next time, I will

_____

_____

SPRING

i. BREAK ROUTINE

A new season is a reminder to let go of the reins every so often to step outside of your day-to-day life.

Taking that brief moment away allows you to recalibrate your mind and your heart and return to your work with more intention and new clarity.

Breaking routine can be big or small. It can mean leaving town and going on a national or international adventure. Or it can be as simple as waking up early one morning rather than sleeping through the alarm, making coffee at home when you normally grab it on the run, or planning a special lunch date with a friend on a day you normally eat at your desk.

THIS WEEK TRY TO DO ONE THING THAT IS OUTSIDE YOUR NORMAL ROUTINE.

Begin by considering: What's your longest-held routine? Could you break it just one time? How would that feel?

_____

_____

_____

_____

_____

_____

Where in your day or your week could you give up a moment
of work for a moment of reflection?

_____

_____

_____

_____

_____

_____

_____

_____

Where in your day or your week could you give up a moment
of work for a moment of fun?

_____

_____

_____

_____

_____

_____

_____

_____

HIT REFRESH AND RESET
YOUR SPIRIT. BREAK
YOUR ROUTINE AND SEE
WHAT TRANSPIRES.

ii. **GROW SOFT**

Normally, we think of power as an outward show of strength, as an accumulation of money and knowledge, as a force to be reckoned with.

This is a phallic power that emphasizes traditionally masculine traits. This power's slogan might be Go Hard, Push Through, Keep Fighting, or Win at All Costs.

Soft power is different. It's power that is cultivated and grows on the inside. It's the strength you shore up in your spirit that shines through your smile as self-assurance.

It's a feminine or feminist power that attempts to redefine the traits we value in society. This power doesn't tell you to go hard; it tells you to grow soft.

> THIS WEEK'S MANTRA
> IS AN EXPLORATION
> OF THE POWER THAT
> COMES THROUGH
> SELF-KNOWLEDGE AND
> VULNERABILITY.

It's a reconsideration of what it means to empower ourselves and others.

It's about attending to each crack in our seams as a potential opening to the world rather than a dangerous flaw.

This will help us break down the walls that keep us from others rather than reinforcing them and building new ones.

What does the word "vulnerability" mean to you?

_____

_____

_____

_____

What examples of vulnerability can you think of?

_____

_____

_____

_____

How does being vulnerable make you feel?

_____

_____

_____

_____

What are ways in which being vulnerable has been helpful in your life?

_____

_____

_____

_____

What are times in which being vulnerable has been hard or bad for you?

_____

_____

_____

What are the spaces where sharing vulnerability feels safe and fosters community?

_____

_____

_____

As we consider soft power this week, I invite you to experiment with growing softer. How might this make you more powerful?

_____

_____

_____

_____

_____

_____

_____

_____

_____

iii. **OPEN DOORS**

What would happen if you opened every door in your life?

All of them.

Every single one you come across.

Like a kid when they go to a friend's house and immediately run around the whole place barging into every room.

This week try signing up for every class that sounds cool, showing up for every event your friends throw, and following up with every neat acquaintance you meet (maybe even some of the ones you met awhile ago and never followed up with).

Put all your feelers out there and coffee-date your heart out.

WE CAN'T DO EVERYTHING ALL THE TIME.

But for a week, we can remember to try new things and follow our gut down those long hallways of life.

So much of adulthood is about making plans to succeed at what's expected or building routines to survive the monotony of daily life.

But like you may have found with the suggestion to break your routines, the real living comes through the doors we throw open on a whim.

Later this year, we'll get back to the reminders that there are also doors in your life that it's really important to shut.

But for now, try opening a few to see where they take you.

Consider:

What's one new thing you could try this week?

_____

_____

_____

_____

_____

_____

What's one conversation you could have that might spark a fresh opportunity?

_____

_____

_____

_____

_____

_____

_____

What's something you haven't done in a long time that you'd like to do again?

_____

_____

_____

_____

_____

_____

_____

_____

How can you make that happen?

_____

_____

_____

_____

_____

_____

_____

_____

_____

_____

iv. **ENACT YOUR EMOTIONS**

One of the most important lessons we can learn from feminist activists and theorists is that feelings matter, and often our most challenging feelings are our most important ones.

Historically, feelings and emotions have been dismissed in favor of reason and rationality.

You can see this in how "crazy" women are written off in favor of "reasonable" men or how women are told to "quit being emotional" when they bring up concerns or show any feelings.

It also shows up in less obviously gendered ways, such as how quantitative statistics are valued over qualitative stories or how credentialed degrees are valued over life experience.

All of these together have led to the logical being valued so much more than the emotional in Western society.

None of this is to say that logic or reason is inherently or necessarily bad. The problem is that logic and reason can do only so much, particularly when it comes to social change.

While big thinking and careful logistics are crucial for mass movements, it's the emotions we share that are going to create the changes that we wish and need to see in the world.

It's feelings in our guts and our hearts that are going to get us out into the streets and starting a revolution.

It's all about how we enact our emotions.

Now, sometimes our emotions enact us straight to the bathtub with a bottle of wine or a carton of ice cream.

But our feelings can do so much more than that.

Our emotions can drive us to protests and letter-writing campaigns and conflict resolution training. They can take us to check on our homeless neighbors and bring supplies to our local animal shelters.

Our emotions need to take us to those places as often as they do to the bathtub.

This week reflect on the following:

Which of your emotions lead you toward other people and into action with them? (Does being angry rile you up the most? Being hurt? Falling in love? Feeling scammed?)

_____

_____

_____

_____

_____

_____

How you can express those emotions with purpose?

_____

_____

_____

_____

_____

_____

What would it look like to channel those feelings into something larger than yourself?

_____

_____

_____

_____

_____

_____

_____

_____

Think of two concrete examples or opportunities for you to do this in the near future. Write them here.

_____

_____

_____

_____

_____

_____

_____

_____

_____

V. **AMPLIFY**

An important aspect of feminist consciousness—particularly for white women—is learning to be an ally.

What does it mean to be an ally exactly?

It means listening and empathizing.

It means seeking out opportunities to hear marginalized voices and paying close attention to what they say.

It means recognizing and accounting for your privilege and understanding the structural and systemic entities that may oppress others.

Once you do that, it means amplifying those voices and making sure they're heard.

In some cases, the voice that needs to be heard may be your own. In other cases, you may need to hold back your opinions and amplify others. Being an ally is about taking the time to listen, learning from what you hear, and discerning whose voice must be amplified based on the situation at hand.

DO THAT WORK, THEN THE PREMISE IS SIMPLE: SHOW UP AND SHOUT.

A few questions to help you begin:

What does being a good listener mean to you?

_____

_____

_____

_____

_____

_____

_____

_____

When was the last time you listened to someone who has different identities from your own tell their story or speak about their perspective?

_____

_____

_____

_____

_____

_____

_____

_____

_____

When was the last time you shared your story or perspective?
And with whom did you share it?

_____

_____

_____

_____

_____

_____

_____

_____

_____

_____

How might you listen more often?

_____

_____

_____

_____

_____

_____

_____

_____

_____

_____

To whom do you want to listen?

_____

_____

_____

_____

_____

_____

How might you speak up more often? (Also consider: should you speak up more often?)

_____

_____

_____

_____

_____

_____

Whom do you want to listen to you?

_____

_____

_____

_____

_____

_____

vi. SHINE YOUR LIGHT

Because of the way that night and day seem to alternate, we tend to think of light and dark as mutually exclusive. It's either night or day, either light or dark, always one or the other. Never both.

In a certain sense, however, this is a fallacy.

It's not that day is light and night is dark but that each rotation of the Earth is the slipping within and between the two, that light and dark mingle in every hour.

This is a hard lesson to hold but one that can bring a lot of peace when embraced.

> THE TASK OF THIS
> WEEK IS TO LEARN
> TO DWELL IN THE
> DARKNESS.

The darkness of not knowing what will come next. The darkness of not knowing how to proceed. The darkness of not being sure who is close to us and how to reach them, let alone how to connect with those who feel (and in reality may be) far away.

The purpose of dwelling in the darkness is to learn to shine our light. Illumination is not the opposite of darkness. Both always go hand in hand.

What places or darknesses have you been avoiding in your life? Can you identify your shadows and spend a little time with them? Use the space below to try. Write about it below.

This may feel hard. Or bad, even. That's OK. It's something that takes time. And right now may not be the right time to do it.

But if you were able to spend some time in the dark, now ask yourself: Did you find any clarity there? Did any light begin to shine?

_____

_____

_____

_____

_____

_____

_____

_____

_____

_____

_____

_____

_____

TAKE A DEEP BREATH
AND BE GENTLE WITH
YOURSELF. AS LIGHT
BEGINS TO SHINE IN
THE DARK, FIND IT.

vii. **CRAFT COMMUNITY**

Our patriarchal capitalist society tells us that we should have a do-it-yourself mentality.

We have to be individuals and accomplish everything on our own. When we succeed, we get all the glory. And when we fail, it's all on us.

But a feminist perspective emphasizes community and the role that others play in all of our decisions and actions.

Our successes and failures belong to the people who love, support, and praise us as much as they belong to any one of us individually.

No single person can do everything. It's never all on us.

That said, one person can craft a network that allows them to create meaningful change with widespread impact.

AN INDIVIDUAL CAN
CHANGE THE WORLD.
BUT THEY'RE NEVER
DOING IT ALONE.

This week meditate on these questions:

Do you have real community in your life?

_____

_____

_____

_____

_____

What does real community mean to you?

_____

_____

_____

_____

_____

Are there women you turn to for advice? For comfort? Who
are they?

_____

_____

_____

_____

_____

How do these women inspire and impress you?

_____

_____

_____

_____

How do you inspire and impress them?

_____

_____

_____

_____

How can you cultivate these relationships?

_____

_____

_____

_____

How can you craft a better community?

_____

_____

_____

_____

viii. **PERSIST**

Giving up is tempting sometimes, isn't it?

Some tasks present so many obstacles that appear so large that abandoning them altogether seems like the only option.

This week's mantra is a reminder that some storms appear large but pass quickly and others we have to ride out for the long haul.

Either way, we'll never know what type of storm we're in unless we persist through it. And we can't see the rainbow until we're on the other side.

P E R S I S T E N C E
T E A C H E S   U S   A B O U T
O U R   S T R E N G T H S .

We learn our true potential when we push past the moments where we want to give up.

What is something you've been struggling with or frustrated about lately? Are you feeling stuck in any area of your life?

Make a list of what comes to mind.

_____

_____

_____

_____

_____

_____

What things on the list seem worth weathering? Which struggles deserve your persistence?

_____

_____

_____

_____

_____

_____

How can you persist in each one a little longer?

_____

_____

_____

_____

_____

What strength will you find on the other side of that moment?

_____

_____

_____

_____

_____

_____

ix. SHARE LOVE

One of the best ways we can resist our white supremacist, capitalist, patriarchal society is to care for, about, and with each other.

> OUR MOST POWERFUL
> TOOL OF RESISTANCE
> IS CULTIVATING LOVE
> AMONG OURSELVES.

In our culture, we often think of love as a romantic grand gesture, but more often it is embedded in small moments of care that we offer to people we do or don't know in our everyday lives.

This week we'll do some work to making those people feel cared for as we share our love with them.

On the left side of the chart below, make a list of people you love.

In the center column, write down one way you've cared for each of those people recently (if you have).

In the right column, brainstorm a way you could express your care or affection for each of those people in the near future.

person you love	one way you've cared for them recently	one way you'll care for them soon

When you're done, review your chart. Whom have you shown love the most often? Whom have you neglected lately? Do any patterns stand out to you? Reflect on them below.

_____

_____

_____

_____

_____

Now we'll repeat the exercise for people you encounter in your daily life who may not be on your list of people you love.

Think about the strangers you engage with and the acquaintances who didn't make your first list. The people on the bus. The barista who makes your coffee. The coworkers across the hall.

Not everyone you interact with daily may be someone you want to love, but it's likely that many of them exist in a more neutral space where you neither truly regard nor disregard them.

Using the chart below, list as many people you encounter in your day-to-day life as you can think of in the left column. Add any ways you've shown them kindness, love, or positive attention in the center column, and brainstorm ways you might show them you care on the right.

person you encounter	something you've done for them	something you will do for them

When you're done, reflect on which of these acts of kindness and gratitude you think you could offer this week and to whom.

_____

_____

_____

_____

_____

_____

After reflecting, make a list on another sheet of paper, and carry it with you through the week.

Check things off as you go.

X. **RETURN HOME**

While we often speak of home as a physical location, sometimes it seems to be more of a feeling.

Home means different things to each of us, but it is almost always a powerful, grounding force.

We all share the earth as our home.

We all tend and care for it and ourselves as inhabitants of this planet.

The task for this week is to find a way to return to the feeling of home.

Maybe you reach out to a person who knew you when you were younger or when you felt most like yourself.

Maybe you visit a part of town you spent a lot of time in when you first lived there.

Maybe you make a meal your mother made you growing up.

Maybe you research spiritual practices of your ancestors.

If nothing comes to mind as home for you or returning to some sense of "home" feels triggering or traumatic, then find a way to return to the earth this week.

Walk barefoot in soil or sand.

Immerse yourself in a body of water.

Stare at the sky in reverence.

Here are a few prompts to help you begin the process of returning home:

Is home a place for you? A feeling? A person? List as many things as you can that feel like home.

_____

_____

_____

_____

_____

_____

_____

_____

_____

_____

_____

_____

_____

_____

_____

_____

_____

_____

_____

_____

_____

How long has it been since you went home? Do you go home every day? Is going home a special occasion?

_____

_____

_____

_____

_____

_____

_____

_____

Home also describes our dwelling places. Do you have a place to rest your head each night? Does where you live right now feel like home?

_____

_____

_____

_____

_____

_____

_____

_____

_____

Do you have more than one home? Maybe the place you live isn't the place you call home. Or you have a chosen family that feels more like home than your biological family. Use the space below to reflect on what it means or how it feels to have many homes.

_____

_____

_____

_____

_____

_____

_____

_____

_____

_____

_____

_____

_____

When you're done, choose one way you'll return home this week. Write it below as a promise to yourself.

_____

_____

_____

_____

xi. DEFINE DESIRE

As humans, we are full of desires. Sunshine. Sex. Pizza. Pets. Community. Fresh air. Clean water. Funny jokes.

We're often taught that the opposite of desire is discipline—that we can control our desires if we're disciplined enough and that if we can't do so, we're gluttonous or lazy or bad.

Many of us are even encouraged to be ascetic, abstaining from bodily pleasure and embracing the life of the mind, taking hold of and limiting our desires to make sure our rational needs constrict our emotional/embodied wants.

> BUT DESIRE IS A DEEPLY EROTIC AND FEMININE POWER. IT IS A RICH RESOURCE AND AN INTUITIVE GUIDE.

Ask yourself: What does the word "erotic" mean to you? Is it sexual? Is it intimate? What emotions do you associate with it? Take a few moments and try to write your own definition of the erotic.

_____

_____

_____

_____

_____

_____

_____

_____

Next, make a list of ways you can get in touch with your erotic self. This list will be deeply personal and unique to you. Be imaginative and creative as you write down possibilities.

In developing a feminist consciousness, our goal is not to quell or repress the erotic but to learn to define what and how we desire.

We shouldn't take control of our desires by limiting them.

We should embrace our desires by learning to articulate them.

This week make a list of things you want.

What do you desire? How specific can you be?

Use the space below to write as many things you desire as you can think of. Be creative. Be imaginative. Be meaningful. Nothing is too big or too small, too unimaginable or too frivolous to make the list.

_____

_____

_____

_____

_____

_____

_____

_____

_____

_____

_____

_____

_____

Now that you've made your list, consider: How can these desires play a larger role in your daily life?

Freewrite below about whatever comes to mind or choose a few specific desires from your list and make a plan for how you'll obtain them.

_____

_____

_____

_____

_____

_____

_____

_____

_____

_____

_____

_____

_____

_____

_____

_____

_____

_____

_____

WRITE YOUR SELF

Throughout history, women have used words to share their experiences and selves.

From Sojourner Truth to Virginia Woolf and from Sylvia Plath to bell hooks, women have turned to language to make sense of their lives and to claim space in the world.

They've used words to speak their bodies and truths aloud, so that they could know and share their experiences in a world that so often diminished them.

HAVE YOU EVER WRITTEN YOUR STORY?

Have you shared a scene or told it from start to finish?

This week we'll take a moment to start that process.

To write a single scene or many scenes.

To start at the beginning or in the middle.

Maybe you'll do this alone at home with pen and paper or in a crowded coffee shop on your laptop.

Maybe you'll start telling the story in conversation with someone you care about or in speech to a room full of people.

No matter how you do it, the goal is to begin writing, because your story is important, and only you can write it.

Below are a few prompts to help. Don't feel pressured to respond to any or all of them. They're only invitations.

When and where did your life begin?

_____

_____

_____

_____

_____

_____

_____

_____

What's a formative experience you remember from your childhood or adolescence?

_____

_____

_____

_____

_____

_____

_____

_____

When did you finally feel like an adult?

_____

_____

_____

_____

_____

_____

_____

_____

_____

Who or what was your first love, your best friend, or your chosen family?"

_____

_____

_____

_____

_____

_____

_____

_____

_____

How would you draw the narrative arc of your story? A mountain? A spiral? A line up or down? Try to illustrate it below.

WRITING YOUR STORY ISN'T A ONE-WEEK PROCESS. BUT AS YOU FIND THE WORDS, REMEMBER: YOUR STORY IS YOURS—TAKE IT.

As you begin writing your story, consider: What are the stories you've been telling yourself about your life? How can you change the narrative to suit you?

_____

_____

_____

_____

_____

_____

_____

_____

_____

_____

_____

_____

_____

_____

_____

xii. **CARRY A TALISMAN**

As spring slips into summer, consider crafting a ritual to associate with the change of season.

What is one thing you hope to accomplish this summer?

_____

_____

_____

_____

_____

_____

_____

_____

What do you hope the universe will provide for you?

_____

_____

_____

_____

_____

_____

_____

_____

_____

_____

Meditate on your answers to these two questions. Does any particular image come to mind? Try to illustrate or describe it below, even if it's just a scribble or a stream of consciousness.

Now find a small talisman to represent this image and the things you hope to manifest in the upcoming season.

Maybe it's a stone or a crystal, a photo or a keychain.

Try to choose something of a size that you can carry with you throughout the summer.

LET IT HOLD YOUR DREAMS.
AND AS THE SEASONS
CHANGE, HOLD IT TIGHT.

SUMMER

i. **REFRESH**

The start of summer marks the apex of the growth season of the year, a full turn from the depth of winter.

You've survived,
maybe even thrived, and there's still so much ahead!

TAKE A FEW MOMENTS
THIS WEEK TO CHECK
IN WITH YOURSELF AND
WHAT YOU NEED FROM THE
UPCOMING MONTHS.

If you're working through this mantra practice chronologically, turn back to your notes from early in the year and see what has shifted.

How were you feeling two seasons ago?

_____

_____

_____

_____

_____

_____

_____

_____

_____

_____

Have you let go of or embraced certain feelings?

_____

_____

_____

_____

_____

_____

_____

_____

_____

What have you learned about yourself?

_____

_____

_____

_____

_____

_____

_____

_____

_____

_____

What have you learned about feminism?

_____

_____

_____

_____

_____

_____

_____

_____

_____

What do you hope is to come?

_____

_____

_____

_____

_____

_____

_____

_____

_____

_____

Write answers to each of these questions, then ask yourself:

What would it mean to hit refresh on your life right now?

_____

_____

_____

_____

Can you identify one area of your life that needs a refresh
the most?

_____

_____

_____

_____

Set a concrete refresh goal and three steps for enacting it.

_____

_____

_____

_____

_____

_____

Write it on a clean sheet of paper and hang it by your desk,
tape it to your mirror, or fold it up to carry in your wallet.

Revisit it next week and see what feels different or the same.

ii. DEMAND FREEDOM

When we think of freedom, many things may come to mind: spiritual freedom, feeling free, political rights, social causes. Freedom refers to many things in our lives.

From a political framework, freedom certainly is an important right to claim and fight for. It's also part of a larger social and economic analysis of power and oppression.

Considering freedom from a feminist framework reminds us that freedom is also an important affective dimension of our lives. Freedom isn't just something enshrined in legal documents or social norms; it's also something we must feel.

This week meditate on what it means to you to feel free in your daily life and your relationships.

Consider the following questions:

What does freedom mean to you?

_____

_____

_____

_____

_____

_____

_____

_____

_____

_____

What does freedom feel like in your gut? Your heart?

_____

_____

_____

_____

_____

_____

_____

_____

_____

_____

What conditions have to be true for you to feel free?

_____

_____

_____

_____

_____

_____

_____

_____

_____

_____

_____

Be gentle yet firm with yourself in this exploration.

What stands out as flexible, and what is nonnegotiable?

_____

_____

_____

_____

What would it mean for you to demand this feeling of freedom?

_____

_____

_____

_____

How can you seek and cultivate freedom in your life?

_____

_____

_____

_____

How can you assist others in their search?

_____

_____

_____

_____

iii. **IMAGINE RADICALLY**

This week imagine what it would be like to take a sharp left in your life.

Is there a dream you've never followed? A person you've never reached out to? A path left untraveled?

What would happen if you turned toward that dream, person, or path?

Write down how you feel just reading those questions.

_____

_____

_____

_____

                _____

                         _____

                         _____

                         _____

                         _____

                         _____

                         _____

Now consider taking that leap.

How would it feel?

Scary, to be sure.

But also invigorating, enlivening, maybe even freeing.

Write down a few more feelings you have as you play the scenario in your mind.

_____

_____

_____

_____

_____

Looking back, when was the last time you made a radical change in your life? Have you ever?

_____

_____

_____

_____

_____

_____

_____

_____

Now turn your attention from things you might wish you chose to things you can't even imagine being yours.

What's something you wish you could have for your future that you don't really believe is possible?

Write down at least one thing.

Dare to articulate that dream.

Then write another unimaginable thing.

Then a few more.

_____

_____

_____

_____

_____

_____

_____

_____

_____

_____

_____

_____

_____

_____

Make a list of how you'd feel if you did or had one or any of those things.

_____

_____

_____

_____

_____

_____

_____

_____

_____

_____

_____

_____

_____

IS JOY ANYWHERE
ON THAT LIST?
CHASE IT.

iv. **FORGIVE**

Forgiveness is a fickle endeavor. It's something we often seek to have or to give, but it seems tenuous and unclear.

Part of the challenge of forgiveness is that forgiveness presupposes that something "wrong" has been done, and the nature of that wrongdoing presupposes that something else "should" have been done.

How do we know what we should do in our own lives or for others?

We often rely on rules and laws to determine these "shoulds."

But how often do we feel like someone has done something wrong without being able to point to the exact rule that's been broken?

This week's mantra is about meditating on the things you believe you should be doing in your life and what you think others around you should be doing.

How can you define those "shoulds" more clearly? Start by making a list of all the things you think you "should" be doing in your life.

_____

_____

_____

_____

_____

_____

Which items on this list can you let go of?

_____

_____

_____

_____

_____

_____

_____

Next, make a list of things you think are unforgiveable.

_____

_____

_____

_____

_____

_____

_____

_____

_____

_____

Choose one and try to imagine forgiving a person who's done that thing. Can you imagine it? What does it feel like?

_____

_____

_____

_____

_____

_____

_____

_____

_____

_____

After completing these exercises, this week focus on forgiving yourself for a slipup or all-out abandonment of those things you think you "should" be doing.

Try to forgive someone else for the same.

The new sense of forgiveness you may find will help you transform your ideas of justice and fairness. Over time it may show you how to invent new boundaries and agreements that you craft intentionally.

This practice makes for better feminists, stronger communities, and richer lives.

V. **RUN WILD**

Women have been associated with the wild for most of human history.

What it means to be feminine is attached to a deeply human sense of embodiment and desire.

To the birth of all life.

To the womb that is the deep, dark space we emerge from but never quite remember.

> THAT'S WHAT THE WILD IS AFTER ALL. A PURELY GENERATIVE DARKNESS.

A space our minds can't quite make sense of and where our bodies take charge.

What images are conjured up when you meditate on the words "run wild"?

_____

_____

_____

_____

_____

_____

_____

_____

How do those images shift when you imagine yourself
running wild?

_____

_____

_____

_____

_____

_____

_____

_____

How do those images change when you imagine women all
over the world running wild?

_____

_____

_____

_____

_____

_____

_____

_____

This week infuse your life with more wildness.

How can you return to that deep, dark space of yourself?

_____

_____

_____

_____

_____

_____

_____

_____

How can you carry that space into the light of the world?

_____

_____

_____

_____

_____

_____

_____

_____

_____

vi. SIT IN THE MESS

Our society places a high value on progress. Everything and everyone should always be moving forward and getting better.

This is a fairly phallic, masculine premise—that everything must be up and pointed ahead all the time.

Life doesn't necessarily work that way.

Nature moves cyclically, circling back around to and through the same four seasons and many moon cycles as time passes.

Because of this societal valuing of the progressive over the cyclical, when something goes awry in life, we tend to work hard to push past it. We want to move forward and move on as quickly as possible.

Sometimes, however, we need to stay in those moments of discomfort.

WE NEED TO LINGER IN THAT SPACE AND SEE HOW IT TAKES SHAPE. WE NEED TO SIT IN THE MESS.

What's one area of your life or the life of someone close to you that may not be going as planned right now?

_____

_____

_____

_____

_____

_____

_____

_____

_____

How do you feel when you are in a good place and someone else isn't or when a friend is in a good place and you aren't?

_____

_____

_____

_____

_____

_____

_____

_____

_____

_____

How can you sit in the mess with yourself or with them?

_____

_____

_____

_____

_____

_____

_____

_____

_____

_____

What can you learn from making space there?

_____

_____

_____

_____

_____

_____

_____

_____

_____

_____

_____

vii. DEVOTE YOURSELF

Famous singer, songwriter, and author Patti Smith titled her book on writing *Devotion*.

Throughout the book, an important theme is the way that writing becomes an all-encompassing task. That it's something we're taken in by and must give ourselves to.

The world we live in, however, is full of distractions. The rise of leisure activities and technologies has filled all our moments with mindless things to do. And each of these things gets in the way of the possibility of devotion.

When was the last time you got caught up in a project or endeavor with such a fervent pleasure that you forgot about everything else? When was the last time you devoted yourself to something so fully that the world beyond it just fell away?

Try to remember that moment and write about it here. What were you doing? Whom were you with? How did it feel? How long did that feeling last? Try to savor and share the details below.

_____

_____

_____

_____

_____

_____

_____

_____

_____

Now that you've remembered what devotion feels like, this week meditate on an idea or dream that you could imagine devoting yourself to.

Maybe it's a book, a business, or a band.

Take the space below to dream for a few moments. Make notes and sketches. Outline steps and processes.

How does it feel to get swept up in those plans?

_____

_____

_____

_____

_____

_____

_____

_____

_____

Could you make them a reality?

_____

_____

_____

_____

_____

_____

_____

_____

_____

_____

viii. BELIEVE IN ABUNDANCE

Living in a capitalist economy means living in a world where our lives are valued by our productive—or, for women, reproductive—abilities. It means judging ourselves and others by how much material wealth we accumulate. It means being a cog in an exploitative system, always exploiter or exploited, often both simultaneously.

In a capitalist system, the prevailing ideology insists that the less of something there is in the world, the more valuable it may become. The more valuable it is, the more we are supposed to want to own it. The more we want to own it, the more we can never have enough.

Because we're told there is never enough, we find ourselves holding too tightly to the things we have, feeling like there's too little and wondering how to get more. We operate from a place of lack. That is called a scarcity mindset.

A scarcity mindset permeates our lives far beyond just our relationship to material possessions. For example, it can lead us to believe that there is a limited amount of love in the world, so we can be deserving of only so much.

TO RESIST A SCARCITY MINDSET, WE NEED TO LEARN TO OPERATE FROM A SPACE OF ABUNDANCE.

We need to look around and realize how often there is plenty.

And then we have to share. And we have to share a little more than we think we can. And trust that it will come back to us in turn.

This is what it means to believe in abundance. To share what you can and a little more.

TO BELIEVE THAT IT WILL RETURN TO YOU, BECAUSE THERE IS PLENTY IN THE WORLD FOR ALL OF US.

The first step in this process is emulating Goldilocks and learning to identify enough by finding too little and too much.

To begin, write about a time when you felt like you had too little. Maybe it was too little money or too little food. Maybe it was too little love or too little joy. How did that feel? Be as specific as you can.

_____

_____

_____

_____

_____

_____

_____

_____

_____

Now write about a time when you had too much. Maybe you ate too much or drank too much. Maybe you knew too much or spoke too much. How did that feel? Again, be as specific as you can.

_____

_____

_____

_____

_____

_____

_____

Having reflected on too little and too much, now try to imagine having enough. Have you ever felt like you had enough? What was the circumstance? What was the feeling? If you can't think of an instance of enough, imagine what enough might feel like. Write or draw your feeling of enough below.

_____

_____

_____

_____

_____

_____

_____

_____

Returning to the present moment, where can you find abundance in your life this week? Write down two or three (or more) areas where you feel you have enough lately.

_____

_____

_____

_____

_____

_____

_____

_____

How can you share that abundance? Brainstorm a few concrete opportunities.

_____

_____

_____

_____

_____

_____

_____

_____

ix. **REST TOGETHER**

Normally, we think of resting as something that happens in solitude.

Rest is sleeping in on a Sunday morning. It's painting your nails or taking a bath.

But sometimes during those times our minds wander back to whatever has been bothering us. Perhaps we mull over negative thoughts or return to painful memories.

So even though we may not be doing anything, we don't actually rest.

Even though we think of rest as a solitary endeavor, it can also be a deeply communal activity.

We can rest together at a yoga class or in a movie theater. We can take long walks with friends or linger on the phone for hours.

Sometimes resting with others allows us to get out of our heads enough for the cobwebs to clear and clarity to take their place.

This week find your people and spend time just spending time with them.

Sit on the couch together chatting about nothing. Linger over a long brunch. Go for a swim. Ask how you can nourish and nurture each other and do those things.

REST TOGETHER AND SEE WHERE THAT QUIET COMMUNITY TAKES YOU.

Allow that rest to motivate you to work harder and better toward your goals, but only after taking a well-deserved break to care for yourself and those around you.

In the space below, list anyone in your life whom you think you could rest with.

_____

_____

_____

_____

_____

_____

_____

_____

Make a list of activities you think could be restful to do together.

_____

_____

_____

_____

_____

_____

_____

After you spend time resting together, use the space below to reflect on how it made you feel.

_____

_____

_____

_____

_____

_____

_____

_____

When you're done, call or text one of those people and make plans.

X. **SET BOUNDARIES**

Our society tends to always be asking us for more. Especially those of us who are women.

We're expected to give our time, our energy, our care, and our attention to everyone all the time. And we're rarely applauded for offering any of those things to ourselves.

In order to resist this, we have to set boundaries, and one helpful way to set boundaries is to develop personal policies.

How do you make personal policies? It's fairly straightforward:

First, come up with a list of things you immediately wish you had said no to every single time you said yes to them.

For example, maybe you always say yes to happy hour, but then every time you regret going and spending $40 right after work.

It can be anything. Feel around for those moments of regret, resentment, or resistance in your life and write about a few of them below.

_____

_____

_____

_____

_____

_____

_____

_____

Now we'll turn that list into a few personal policies . For example, with the scenario above, I might write:

- I have a personal policy against going out for drinks after work before I've had a chance to go home first.

- Or, I have a personal policy against going to happy hour spots where the drinks cost more than $10.

The exact personal policy you develop is flexible, but what's important is that you use personal policies to set boundaries that (a) eliminate anxiety and (b) help you move toward your goals and happiness in life.

The trick for using personal policies is to develop them in advance and to always say that they're personal policies when you use them; for example, "No, thank you. I have a personal policy against . . ."

So when your coworker asks you to head out of work at 4:45 p.m. to go to that new happy hour spot with $18 cocktails, you can say:

- "No, thank you. I have a personal policy against going out before I've had a chance to go home first."

- Or, "No, thank you. I have a personal policy against spending that much on a happy hour drink."

It can be hard to say at first, but personal policies incite respect for boundary setting and strength. You may feel a bit awkward, but people will be impressed!

This week spend some time brainstorming a list of new personal policies. They don't have to be about happy hours like this example. Start with the list you just made and expand from there.

Make sure to start each item with "I have a personal policy against . . ." to make your statement as potent as possible.

_____

_____

_____

_____

_____

_____

_____

_____

_____

_____

_____

_____

_____

_____

_____

_____

_____

_____

_____

Now pick one or two to put into action. You won't regret it.

xi. **LABOR LESS**

Did you know the word "labor" entered the English language in the thirteenth century, but the phrase "labor of love" didn't appear until 1797?

The idea of a person "going into labor" in childbirth appeared in the fifteenth century (although only in connection to the sense of suffering in the French word "travail").

The idea of a "labor union" emerged in the mid-nineteenth century, and the first U.S. Labor Day was celebrated in 1882.

All of this is to say that it's no wonder our sense of life, love, gender, community, self-worth, and sex is all tied up in really complicated conversations around labor and work.

Labor can invite birth and death in the same breath, and under capitalism we find its conditions ever demanding.

This mantra is an invitation to pause and reflect on where your work feels bountiful and where it feels laborious without benefit.

Are you working too much? Too little? How do you feel about work lately?

_____

_____

_____

_____

_____

_____

_____

Remember that labor isn't just your "job."

Are you laboring for wealth? Health? Friends? Family? What kinds of labor are you doing lately?

_____

_____

_____

_____

_____

_____

_____

_____

_____

In contrast, what aspects of your life don't feel like work? What makes those things different?

_____

_____

_____

_____

_____

_____

_____

_____

_____

How can you lean into those places and spaces that don't feel like work?

_____

_____

_____

_____

_____

_____

_____

_____

If at any point in your reflection something feels "too much," meditate on how you can labor less in that area. Write any ideas below.

_____

_____

_____

_____

_____

_____

_____

_____

One way to labor less is to invite community into your work. How could you do that? What respite, mutual aid, and advancement could that provide?

_____

_____

_____

_____

_____

_____

_____

_____

After reflecting on the prompts here, reconsider: What does "labor less" mean to you?

_____

_____

_____

_____

_____

_____

_____

_____

_____

xii. SEEK CRITIQUE

An important part of feminist consciousness is the development of our feminine and feminist selves, the embracing of aspects of our lives and humanity that are crushed by a patriarchal society.

An equally important part of feminist consciousness is also being open to feedback on how we can do better, particularly how we can be better community members and allies.

This week find small ways to seek feedback on your ideas and actions.

Consider: Where are a few places in your life that you might need or want some feedback? Maybe it's in your work or your relationships. Maybe it's in your creative practice or your activism. Make a list of possibilities below.

_____

_____

_____

_____

_____

_____

_____

_____

_____

Thinking of the list you just made, what types of feedback would you find helpful? Are there methods or modes of feedback that you know work best (or worst) for you?

_____

_____

_____

_____

_____

_____

_____

When you're ready to seek feedback, approach these conversations from a vulnerable place and be open to what you hear.

What are feelings (e.g., vulnerability, gratitude, love) you'd like to keep close when you're hearing feedback? List at least a half dozen below.

_____

_____

_____

_____

_____

_____

_____

In seeking feedback, it's also important to identify people who will offer critique from a place of care rather than malice.

Make a list of these caring people now. Consider what makes each of their perspectives unique or important for you to hear. Write their names and list these qualities below.

_____

_____

_____

_____

_____

_____

_____

_____

_____

_____

_____

_____

When you're ready, arrange a space and time to talk.

Review your reflections on how you want to feel during the process before you begin. Take notes during or after you speak.

TAKE A DEEP BREATH WHEN YOU'RE DONE. THEN TAKE THEIR WORDS TO HEART.

xiii. SET NEW PATTERNS

As humans, we seem to develop habits and routines.

We go through our day-to-day lives speaking to the same people, driving the same routes, and visiting the same places.

There's a lot of comfort in these habits and routines.

They help us cope with the scary invariability of the world we live in that often seems chaotic and overwhelming.

But our habits and routines can also be enticing forms of comfort that keep us from growing and fulfilling our potentials.

They can keep us stuck in states we may not intentionally be entering.

This week meditate on what habits and routines you hold fast to in your life.

Do you have coffee every morning? Do you park in the same place each day at work?

Think about how you move through your days. Use the space below to list habits you notice.

_____

_____

_____

_____

_____

_____

_____

_____

When you're more conscious of the habits you have, consider what could change.

Could you become a tea drinker two days a week? Might you walk to work or park your car elsewhere?

Of the habits you listed on the previous page, which ones might you change? Where can you invite new patterns into your life? List a few possibilities below.

_____

_____

_____

_____

_____

_____

_____

_____

_____

_____

_____

_____

_____

_____

_____

_____

From this list, choose at least one routine to experiment with this week. Try something new. See how it feels.

After completing your experiment, check back in here. How did it feel? Do you want to keep experimenting or return to your routine? Write any reflections below.

_____

_____

_____

_____

_____

_____

_____

_____

_____

_____

_____

_____

_____

_____

_____

_____

_____

FALL

i. **ASK**

Our culture places a high value on self-sufficiency. We're supposed to do everything ourselves.

Community, according to our society, is just a plus, something we find if we're lucky.

It may be counterintuitive, then, that one of the best ways to build community is to ask people to help.

When asking for help, you have to come from a place of vulnerability and care, a place of trust in yourself and the other person or people.

Within each ask, there should be an offer embedded: the offer of care and gratitude, of joining a community larger than oneself in which both the one who asks and the one who helps finds fulfillment.

If you ask in this way, people want to help and offer support. They want to come together to assist you.

Consider: Are you the kind of person who asks for help? When was the last time you did so?

_____

_____

_____

_____

_____

_____

_____

This week think about something you could use help with. Write down one or more of those things.

_____

_____

_____

_____

_____

_____

_____

Now, whom can you ask for help, and how can you ask them?

_____

_____

_____

_____

_____

_____

_____

As you consider whom and how you might ask, what can be your offer in return? Think less of making a literal offer (I will do that for you if you will do this for me) and more of the energetic, communal exchange that may take place.

Toward the end of the week, check back in here and answer the questions on the following pages.

What did you end up asking for and from whom?

_____

_____

_____

_____

_____

_____

How did asking make you feel?

_____

_____

_____

_____

Were they able to help you? Did they decline?

_____

_____

_____

_____

How did their response make you feel?

_____

_____

_____

_____

What were you able to offer in return for asking? Was it accepted or declined? How did that make you feel?

_____

_____

_____

_____

_____

_____

_____

_____

What's one larger lesson you can take away about asking?

_____

_____

_____

_____

_____

_____

_____

_____

_____

_____

ii. **EVOLVE**

As fall takes hold of the world, reflect on what aspects of your own life still feel fresh and green and which are feeling wilted.

The process of the world changing seasons is much like the process of our self-evolution over a lifetime.

Sometimes evolving is graceful, and the things we've outgrown fade and fall like leaves from trees.

But other times, the process of evolving can be painful, like repotting a plant that loves its container, resulting in it withering and almost dying.

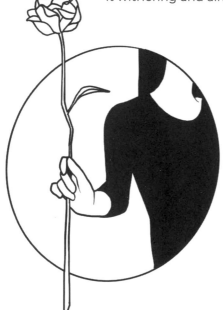

W H A T ' S
I M P O R T A N T   T O
R E M E M B E R   I S
T H A T   T R U E
F L O U R I S H I N G
I S   O N   T H E
O T H E R   S I D E .

Take some time this week to meditate on what pillars in your life may be holding you in place and not allowing you to grow.

Consider: How have you grown this year? What feels new and different?

In contrast, does anything feel rather stale? Are there people, places, or things you've outgrown?

Upon reflection, can you afford to let them go? Or to change your relationship with them? Imagine your biggest, best, most abundant life. Are those things (or the version of you that those things require) a part of it?

_____

_____

_____

_____

_____

_____

_____

_____

_____

_____

_____

_____

_____

_____

_____

_____

_____

_____

When you're done writing, take a deep breath. Evolving is a slow process.

YOU'RE DOING GREAT.

iii. **RECONNECT**

Life is often busy and brutal, and it's easy to lose touch with people we care about.

But relationships are important. Personally and politically.

We need to be touched and heard and held. And the bonds we maintain are our strongest resistance to the neoliberal, capitalist world that isolates us and pits us (especially women) against each other.

This week's mantra is a reminder to reach out to someone whom you may have lost touch with. It's an invitation to reconnect and rekindle.

Begin by making a list of people you'd love to speak to soon. If you can't think of folks you've lost touch with, make a list of people you've never been as close with as you'd like. Write their names below.

_____

_____

_____

_____

_____

_____

_____

_____

_____

_____

Now brainstorm how you might reconnect with them. You could give them a call. Write them an email. Send a small gift. List ideas below.

_____

_____

_____

_____

_____

_____

_____

_____

_____

_____

_____

_____

_____

_____

When you reconnect, tell them what they mean to you in big or small ways. Make a plan for keeping in touch in the future.

BUILD AND REBUILD THE TIES
THAT BIND US TOGETHER.
STRENGTHEN OUR POWERS
OF CARE AND RESISTANCE.

iv. **KNOW YOUR POWER**

Have you embraced the power pose?

Hands on hips. Feet slightly wider than hip width apart. Chest out. Head tilted to the sky.

Try it now. Stand up and power pose.

Hold the position for thirty seconds at least. How does it feel?

_____

_____

_____

_____

_____

_____

This week's task is to reflect on how powerful you are.

Consider these questions:

How does the word "power" make you feel?

_____

_____

_____

_____

_____

_____

What makes you feel powerful, and when do you feel powerful?

_____

_____

_____

_____

_____

_____

_____

_____

_____

What makes you feel powerful?

_____

_____

_____

_____

_____

_____

_____

_____

_____

What groups, in our society, do you think have power?

_____

_____

_____

_____

_____

What qualities do you think a powerful man has?

_____

_____

_____

_____

_____

What qualities do you think a powerful woman has?

_____

_____

_____

_____

_____

_____

Who are powerful people you admire? How many can you list?

_____

_____

_____

_____

_____

_____

_____

_____

Imagine yourself as powerful. How would you describe
yourself in power?

_____

_____

_____

_____

_____

_____

_____

_____

_____

_____

What makes your power uniquely your own?

_____

_____

_____

_____

_____

_____

_____

_____

Carry this final question with you throughout the week.

Take note of the moments you feel powerful

How you can cultivate more of those moments in your life?

_____

_____

_____

_____

_____

_____

_____

_____

_____

v. **NEST**

Associating femininity with domesticity has been one of the most powerfully oppressive tools of our patriarchal society.

We're told that women are supposed to be quiet, toe the line, and stay home. That's their place.

In an effort to rebuke this argument, feminists have fought hard for women's rights to leave home and seek success in the world.

Over the past two centuries, women have begun to liberate themselves from the cult of domesticity, and feminists are still doing important work to maintain and extend women's newfound and hard-earned rights.

Somehow in this fight, however, domesticity became maligned, and the home became a contested space.

In leaving their homes, women also often lost their homes. Space became strange.

This week's mantra invites you to come full circle by simultaneously embracing being liberated from domesticity and cultivating a private space.

FIND A PLACE FOR YOURSELF THIS WEEK AND MAKE IT YOUR OWN.

It can be a physical space or a digital space. It can be at home or at work. Your veritable "room of one's own" can be anywhere—as long as it's your own.

How can you take on a project that will make somewhere feel more like home to you?

Use the space below to collect ideas. Dream as big as major home renovations and as small as cleaning off your desk. List as many things as you can imagine.

_____

_____

_____

_____

_____

_____

_____

_____

_____

_____

_____

_____

_____

_____

_____

_____

_____

_____

_____

_____

After you make the list, choose one or two things you can do this week. If nothing on your list feels doable this week, then add to the list until something feels possible.

After you've done those things, return to this space to reflect.

144 How did taking time to nest impact your mental and physical well-being?

_____

_____

_____

_____

_____

_____

_____

_____

_____

_____

_____

_____

_____

_____

_____

_____

vi. **MAKE MAGIC**

There is a long history of femininity being associated with magic.

In some eras, this gave women great political power; in others, it led to their violent deaths.

No matter the political or historical differences, women's association with magic reflects a general cultural consciousness of a deeply mysterious and deeply feminine power in the world that emanates from Mother Earth and takes root in every human.

Making magic means embracing the unknown in life, stepping into the darkness with courage, and trusting that the world will send you what you need.

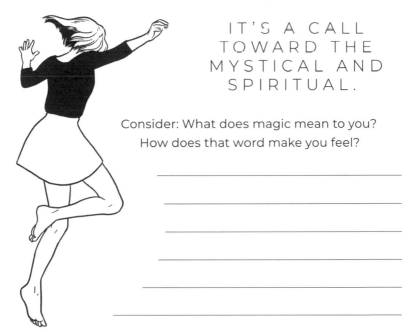

IT'S A CALL TOWARD THE MYSTICAL AND SPIRITUAL.

Consider: What does magic mean to you? How does that word make you feel?

_____

_____

_____

_____

_____

_____

Do you consider yourself a magical person? Do you have any magical practices? (Remember that anything can be magic if you think it is.)

_____

_____

_____

_____

_____

_____

_____

This week seek knowledge that comes from a mystical place.

Check in with your horoscope. Attend a religious ceremony. Have your aura read. Ask a friend to do a tarot reading.

What's something magical you could do this week? Make a list below.

_____

_____

_____

_____

_____

_____

_____

_____

Don't let the bright light of modern science make you turn away from the darkness.

Instead, embrace its power and tap into the strength of our feminine ancestors.

Can you name any historical witches? What magical women do you admire? Write their names (and stories, if you like) below.

_____

_____

_____

_____

_____

_____

_____

_____

_____

After making your list, channel their voices into your own. Summon their strength and celebrate their soft power.

TAKE TIME THIS WEEK
TO CLAIM THE HEALING
YOU DESERVE.

MAKE MAGIC.

vii. **EMBRACE VULNERABILITY**

Have you ever looked up synonyms for vulnerability?

The thesaurus lists the following: defenseless, exposed, liable, unsafe, weak, naked, unguarded, sucker. These words all have negative connotations and meanings.

But vulnerability is a beautiful thing. It's the unique joy of letting your guard down. It allows relationships to flourish. It bonds us deeply together.

Vulnerability is also a quality often associated with femininity. As a result, societal perceptions of women (and even our own identities) often get caught in the tension between these negative and positive senses of the word.

Society tells us that women are more vulnerable than men and that they must act accordingly.

And while it is important to note the real dangers that women face in a society that sees their bodies as assailable, sexualized objects, it is also important to refuse the negative connotations that then get assigned to words like "vulnerability."

WE HAVE TO REWRITE THE DICTIONARIES THAT TELL US THAT FEMININE QUALITIES ARE WEAK AND MAKE US DEFENSELESS.

We have to make the world see that those qualities are our greatest strengths. And doing that starts with experiencing them as strengths ourselves.

So this week challenge yourself to say something, share something, or do something that makes you feel vulnerable.

Here are a few prompts to help you begin:

What does "vulnerability" mean to you?

_____

_____

_____

_____

_____

_____

_____

When was the last time you remember being vulnerable? How did it make you feel?

_____

_____

_____

_____

_____

_____

_____

What are a few ways you could be more vulnerable this week?

_____

_____

_____

_____

_____

_____

_____

_____

How would doing one or more of those things make you feel?

_____

_____

_____

_____

_____

_____

_____

_____

_____

RECOGNIZE EMOTIONAL LABOR

One important feminist effort is to make visible the forms of invisible labor that women (and others) do in their personal and professional lives.

This labor is often called "emotional labor."

Examples of invisible and emotional labor include:

- calmly helping your overbearing manager through employee issues because they feel like they can talk to you

- anxiously handling twice as many emails as a peer because people feel like you're more "approachable"

- being expected to cheerfully host an overwhelming office event because "women are good at those sorts of things."

This week try to keep track of your emotional labor and the invisible or unnoticed labor of women around you.

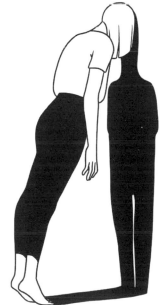

Note the things you do that are crucial to keep so many things running but often get swept under the rug. Pay attention to when you modify your feelings to make someone else feel better or more appreciated. Write about them below.

_____

_____

_____

_____

_____

_____

_____

_____

_____

_____

_____

_____

_____

_____

_____

_____

_____

_____

_____

After making your list, consider: how can you make that labor more visible?

_____

_____

_____

_____

_____

_____

_____

_____

Do you have allies in your work and life who can help you recognize that labor publicly?

_____

_____

_____

_____

_____

_____

_____

_____

_____

Is it an option to stop doing those things, and how might you stop? If it's not an option to stop (it won't be for everyone), how might you feel more appreciated or empowered in those tasks?

ix. **TAKE A DEEP BREATH**

Take a deep breath right now. Inhale. Exhale. Inhale again.
Exhale again. How does it feel? Reflect on those breaths below.

HOW DOES IT FEEL?

_____

_____

_____

_____

_____

_____

What words do you have to describe your own breath? Is it
smooth, even, or shallow? Write all the words you can think of
to describe your breathing.

_____

_____

_____

_____

_____

_____

_____

_____

Close your eyes and take a few more breaths. Focus on your breathing and try to visualize it. Does it look like waves? It is loud like a lion?

Take a moment to breathe, then draw whatever image appears below.

Breathing is an incredibly crucial but entirely mundane aspect of our lives. As such, we often forget about it.

This week try to focus on your breath at different points throughout your day.

Is it slower in the morning?

Does it get more shallow when you drink three cups of coffee?

Use the space below to make notes about what you find.

_____

_____

_____

_____

_____

_____

_____

_____

If focusing on your breath felt good to you, you can find more breathwork tools in the resource list at the end of the book. If not, that's OK. Don't worry about it for today, just . . .

DON'T FORGET TO BREATHE.

x. **GIVE THANKS**

This week's mantra is sweet and simple, and it's all about giving thanks.

Who are the people in your life you're thankful for?

Why do you appreciate them?

How can you thank them?

Use the chart below to answer these questions. List as many people as you can think of in the left column. Share why you're grateful for them in the center column. And list at least one way you can thank them in the right column.

person or people	why you're grateful	how you'll thank them

After you fill out the chart, choose a few names that stand out to you.

Sometime this week, do one of the things you thought of to thank them.

Give thanks for them and give them your thanks.

xi. **CULTIVATE STILLNESS**

Our culture tends to suggest that we should always be on the move.

We value active minds and bodies in motion. Stillness and slowness are branded as dull and lazy.

But what if we refused those associations?

We can challenge the cultural idea that we must always be progressing in favor of finding peace in staying in place.

Consider: Do you often find your mind flitting from place to place unable to focus? Does it wander every time you have a free moment? When was the last time you had trouble focusing?

_____

_____

_____

_____

_____

_____

_____

_____

_____

_____

What about your body? Do your legs twitch as you sit at your desk or your hands wander as you try to type? How does distraction feel in your body?

_____

_____

_____

_____

_____

_____

_____

_____

_____

_____

When was the last time you felt you were truly still?

_____

_____

_____

_____

_____

_____

_____

_____

_____

Take a few moments this week to sit still.

Maybe you find a local yoga or meditation class.

Maybe you make time to sit in the dark each morning.

How does it feel?

_____

_____

_____

_____

_____

_____

_____

_____

_____

_____

_____

_____

_____

FIND A STILLNESS IN
YOUR BODY THAT YOUR
MIND CAN FOLLOW.

xii. **CLOSE DOORS**

As this season comes to a close, it's important to reflect on what else in your life may naturally be coming to an end.

Think about your work, your friendships, your personal projects.

What seems to be wrapping up?

What is finishing right now, or what can you bring to a finish?

Take some time to write answers to these questions.

_____

_____

_____

_____

_____

_____

_____

_____

_____

_____

_____

_____

_____

_____

_____

_____

You need to close a few doors now so that you can open new ones in the future. (Remember the mantra "open doors" from the spring.)

What doors in your life do you want or need to close?

_____

_____

_____

_____

_____

_____

How would that feel?

_____

_____

_____

_____

_____

_____

WHEN THE NEW SEASON
BEGINS, IT WILL BE IMPORTANT
TO HAVE ENOUGH SPACE
IN YOUR LIFE FOR NEW
IDEAS AND POSSIBILITIES.

xiii. CREATE IN THE DARK

In trying times, there's more darkness in the world.

Darkness seems terrifying and intimidating. But if you're at the end of this book, that means you've spent a year learning darkness's deep, feminine power.

What have you learned from leaning into the darkness this past year?

_____

_____

_____

_____

_____

_____

_____

_____

_____

_____

How can you walk into the darkness as the year ends?

_____

_____

_____

_____

_____

_____

_____

What will you bring back to the light?

_____

_____

_____

_____

_____

_____

_____

_____

CLOSING

In preparing this book, I wrote a feminist mantra every Monday for over a year. When I sat down to compile and edit this volume, I was amazed at how quickly I was able to revise old mantras and write new ones. It felt like in my year of writing, I had built up my "mantra muscle," and the meditations came faster and easier than they did in the beginning.

If you've worked through this book, then you've strengthened your mantra muscle as well.

You've reflected on your feminine and feminist self and, hopefully, come to enlightening and empowering conclusions.

If you've been reflecting on one mantra per week, then it's just two weeks until the end of the year. Take these two weeks to reflect and prepare your mantra practice for the future.

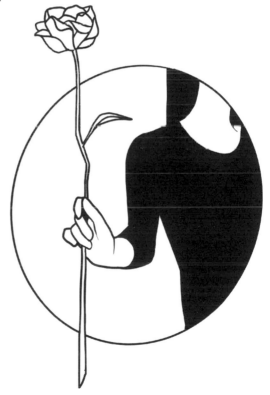

Read back through some of your notes from the earliest mantras, then some from the middle of the book, and a few from the end. What has changed? What have you learned? What do you know or believe about feminism that maybe you didn't at the beginning of your mantra practice?

_____

_____

_____

_____

_____

_____

_____

_____

_____

_____

_____

_____

_____

_____

As you worked through this book, the mantras invited you to consider (and reconsider) how cultivating values such as empathy, community, imagination, intuition, pleasure, joy, and soft power could radically disrupt the power of patriarchy, white supremacy, and capitalism.

Now that you've meditated on these fifty feminist mantras and done the corresponding activities, make your own list of feminist values. What themes do you see in the prompts and your reflections on them? What might be missing or needs to be added? What feminist values are important to you? Why?

_____

_____

_____

_____

_____

_____

_____

_____

_____

_____

_____

_____

_____

_____

_____

_____

_____

_____

What do you know or believe about yourself that maybe you didn't at the start?

_____

_____

_____

_____

_____

_____

_____

_____

_____

_____

_____

_____

Before you move into the new year, practice writing a few mantras for yourself here.

Maybe you write a mantra for the next week, month, and season. Maybe you write a mantra for winter, spring, summer, and fall. Maybe you allow your mind to wander and see what words come.

Try to find words that suit your intentions. Focus on verbs that can guide your actions.

Use the space below to copy your favorite mantras from this year and brainstorm new ones. Choose one or a few to be the themes of the next year. Start chanting them daily.

Writing mantras has been a part of my feminist practice for four years now, and sharing what I've learned from it is deeply important to me.

Thank you for joining me on this journey in feminist community. It's a joy to guide and travel beside you, and I'd love to stay in touch.

Please share your experiences with the mantras on Instagram or Twitter with the hashtag #FiftyFeministMantras, or find me on my website anytime at ameliahruby.com.

All my feminine and feminist love,

(in no particular order)

Sister Outsider: Essays and Speeches, Audre Lorde

Feminism Is for Everybody: Passionate Politics, bell hooks

The Art of Asking: How I Learned to Stop Worrying and Let People Help, Amanda Palmer

A Field Guide to Getting Lost, Rebecca Solnit

Tiny Beautiful Things: Advice on Love and Life from Dear Sugar, Cheryl Strayed

Selected Poems II, Margaret Atwood

Just Kids, Patti Smith

Devotion (Why I Write), Patti Smith

Trying to Make the Personal Political: Feminism and Consciousness-Raising, Half Letter Press

"The Laugh of the Medusa," Helene Cixous

Women Who Run with the Wolves: Myths and Stories of the Wild Woman Archetype, Clarissa Pinkola Estés, PhD

Proposals for the Feminine Economy, Jennifer Armbrust

Feminism for the 99%: A Manifesto, Cinzia Arruzza, Tithi Bhattacharya, and Nancy Fraser

Turn This World Inside Out: The Emergence of Nurturance Culture, Nora Samaran

I'm Afraid of Men, Vivek Shraya

Living a Feminist Life, Sara Ahmed

How to Breathe: 25 Simple Practices for Calm, Joy, and Resilience, Ashley Neese

How to Not Always Be Working: A Toolkit for Creativity and Radical Self-Care, Marlee Grace

A Thousand Mornings: Poems, Mary Oliver

Am I There Yet? The Loop-de-Loop, Zigzagging Journey to Adulthood, Mari Andrew

Little Book of Life Hacks: How to Make Your Life Happier, Healthier, and More Beautiful, Yumi Sakugawa

Self Care in Uncertain Times, Maribeth Helen Keane

Witches, Witch-Hunting, and Women, Silvia Federici

Your Body Is Not an Apology: The Power of Radical Self-Love, Sonya Renee Taylor

The Argonauts, Maggie Nelson

Redefining Realness: My Path to Womanhood, Identity, Love & So Much More, Janet Mock

Care Work: Dreaming Disability Justice, Leah Lakshmi Piepzna-Samarasinha

Pleasure Activism: The Politics of Feeling Good, adrienne maree brown

178   ACKNOWLEDGMENTS

All my love to my friends, family, and followers who supported this project. Special thanks to Emily Jaynes for the amazing illustrations and cover design. Particular appreciation to my partner, JJ, and my cat companion, Wilco.

This book would not exist if my amazing editor, Charlie Upchurch, hadn't rescued it from the internet, and I cannot thank her and my agent, Coleen O'Shea, enough for their help bringing these pages to life.

Photo credit Anna Zajac

Amelia Hruby writes, podcasts, and builds communities of powerful women in Chicago, Illinois. Find her on the internet at @ameliajohruby or ameliahruby.com.